RECKONING WITH DUST

RECKONING WITH DUST

JENNIFER PIRECKI

*May these stories of
strength and
resilience remind
you of your own.*

‡

Redfern Ink
Franklin, Tennessee

Published by Redfern Ink
P O Box 15
Franklin, Tennessee 37065

Published in the United States of America

ISBN 978-0-9994690-0-2

Library of Congress Control Number
2017915171

1. Spirituality and Religion   2. Spiritual Growth

FOR MY FATHER

☦

"He remembers our frame; He remembers that we are dust."

~ David, the Psalmist

CONTENTS

PROLOGUE

I am a child, age 4 or 5. My Grandpa Cheatle, who lives nearby, paints a Bambi-like fawn in repose on a light blue plaque. On the back, he pencils a scripture verse still vivid after forty years, "God careth for you." What does he see? What does he hear? Maybe too much.

Maybe he sees the strain of war weighing heavy on my father. Maybe a window is open and he can hear my parents screaming like I can. Maybe he sees my exhausted mother after retrieving my father from the train station. Not the station close to our home that he misses, but the one two hours away. He is passed out from a 3-martini lunch that day. My brother is crying in the car and I am trying to calm him. Maybe this is what Grandpa sees.

I am 6 or 7. We have moved to the suburbs and are invited to church on Father's Day. My father attends my Sunday School class and we memorize a verse of scripture together—"Be strong and of good courage, be not afraid, for the Lord your God is with you wherever you shall go." We recite it in the church service that follows. Even though it is temporary, it is sweet relief that my family is changing course.

I am 9 or so. We are now living in the flatland of Illinois so my father can attend Seminary. He is to become a pastor—he has been called. He is student, househusband, primary caregiver. Mom is a nurse in an institution close by. She is holding on to the promised benefits of becoming a pastor's wife. The heaviness of war seems lighter. There's no fighting now, at least not the screaming kind that woke me up before.

Prologue

I am 12. We live in the flattest land yet—rural Minnesota. My father's first church brought us here. My mother is pregnant. I am angry because now I have moved towards the front lines of our family's experience and I can see and feel too much. The four of us are stretched by life.

I am the good kind of pastor's daughter. I exhibit a talent for music, so each Sunday a path is worn between piano and pulpit. I am the standard-bearer for all others' children. I am the apple of my father's eye and his good soldier. From my weekly pulpit perch, I can see those that give him a hard time—the critics, the ones responsible for his harshness, his exhaustion, and his stern countenance too. I want to fight his battles for him, I keep looking for ways to help carry his weight.

I am 14. We move back to our hometown where the odyssey of my father's ministry began. I am angry, as I have to start my sophomore year at a new high school. First boyfriends, first heartbreaks. My father redeploys his military intelligence skills by stalking around town to make sure I am not getting into trouble. I fear him too much to cross him.

For once I am busy with my own life—I make good grades, I play volleyball, star in the school musical, and have a few cherished friends. I am too afraid to be rebellious. I keep my anger down by being good.

I am 22. I am leaving home for Nashville. I have completed college with a music degree. An idyllic time. I meet the love of my life within weeks of arriving in Tennessee.

Prologue

I am 24 and newly married. I find my way into church life, although it is different. I am no longer known as a pastor's daughter. Now I have to be my own person. I am grappling with this across every sphere of life.

Under the guise of a visit, my father deposits my mother and sister with me. This is merely a part of his larger decision to leave the family, his marriage, the ministry—a complete break. As the frenzy unfolds, I talk with him, but his is not a voice I know; it is someone who has replaced my father. My father is gone.

I am livid. He has dumped the family. Everything is in question—our past, our faith, our family, their marriage. He is gone and has left me to pick up the pieces. He knows I can, but this is not the battle I wanted to fight for him.

My father returns. He faces all sorts of consequences. He tries to make amends and repairs what he can. It breaks him and it remakes him. He is beloved for his softening. But my mother's resentment will remain until the day he dies.

I am 29. I miscarry my first and only pregnancy. I am awash in hormones and I feel myself unraveling. I am riddled with conflict. And I am confused. Did God change His mind? I have done something oh. so. wrong. But I have been the good girl!

I go to therapy for the first time, which means I am a complete and utter failure. Whoever I've been is evaporating and hopelessness is filling the void. No amount of bootstrapping or spiritual platitudes brings comfort or help. There is a bit of relief that mixes with my dread because it seems like my therapist understands. This is enough for me to hold on for now.

Prologue

I am 30. I have had a difficult therapy session. Words like enmeshment, spiritual distortion, emotional incest. Inflammatory words, accurate words. I leave this session crest fallen and devastated. I am afraid I cannot bear up under the weight of more responsibility.

I leave the session and am in my car. I cannot lift my head off the steering wheel. My eyes are closed and I hear a voice. But I see it too. It's in my head, in my mind's eye. "This is what I came to face."

Something new is emerging from all of this—a suturing inside—a healing of the inner emotional bleed. I am forced to consider a new way of being and believing. I enter graduate school to become a therapist. I study the scriptures, but I am seeing them through a different lens. I want to understand the humanity of Jesus, I want to know how he moved through this life. I need my faith to be a different kind of resource for living than it was before.

I am 35. My father dies suddenly. I am lost without the mirror of my self, it shattered when his heart broke open. Once again, his departure upends my family. We are never the same. I feel the weight of what he left unfinished, but know I cannot fight those battles. The drama surrounding his death continues to trickle into the years that follow. Only in his absence can we see how he held us all together.

I am 47. I have celebrated twenty-three years of marriage and I have been in private practice as a therapist for sixteen years. I am no different from my clients. I have lost what they have lost. I try to keep a microscope on myself so as not to hinder the work, their work—it is sacred terrain.

Prologue

I am a therapist-client-seeker who has studied Jesus' humanity as a way of understanding and examining my own humanity and that of my clients. Emotional and spiritual health are rare and His life embodies both.

I am hopeful that these stories told in the first person narrative will draw attention to the human experiences that affect us all and are timeless in their teachings. That they will help us to learn better how to live through our own reckonings and hold true to who we are meant to be. Like He did.

‡

JACOB

I am Jacob

I stand at the edge of my abyss and You taunt me with a night-visitor. Is it not enough that I must pass through enemy lands? That I have sent my family ahead to be slaughtered by my twin? Twenty years are as the day of my swindling—the long awaited prey trips his snare of hatred.

Was it not enough to have endured Uncle's scheming as a reward for my own? Stolen are the years with my beloved Rachel—absorbed by youthful longing unfulfilled. Laban tainted all that was pure—even my flocks bear the marks of his stealth.

Is it not enough that Father's disdain for me travels with him to his grave? Mother, a pariah, having ransomed her future for the belief that what was Esau's was mine. Her betrayal killed whatever remained of Father's love. These deceits ravage me and still You have me meet my brother.

You think YourSelf a stronger foe than my Esau? Think again; formation of fingerprints came second to my wiry grip. Muscle before flesh, cunning before consciousness—this life is welcome misery compared to our confinement within Mother's womb.

I am Israel, so You say. My prize: a name change. My trophy: a limp. Injured and hobbling, perhaps now Esau will take pity on my unraveled state. I have no fight, nothing left to spend but my humiliation. My infirmity veils all but my next step. I steady myself, for I am at the mercy of what is to come.

I AM

I see you, disillusioned Jacob; stretched to the brink of breaking.

Pulled too tight, your rage will inflame your brother. What you cannot see: Esau is waiting to welcome you and dispel your differences. He is strong but fickle. This rivalry must end so that your futures can unfold. Your body will give way under its opponent tonight, a foreshadowing of what would have been without My intervention. Your days of deceit have come to a close.

As always, you rise to your challenge. With stubborn might you defeat your threat. However, My purpose is Beyond and Within. Your blessed injury plays its part, releasing your fight, your flight. Despite your victory, you contend with your unsteady gait; vulnerable but sturdy. You will relearn to walk, and in due course, you will relearn your Self. Your fire will be used for other things. For now, your broken body leads your way.

I Am Sent

To the river's edge I travel to meet the wily Jacob. Disrupting rare moments of solitude, my chosen strategy is a dream-like ambush. He has wrestled with life more than he has done anything, so he will not go quietly. I am not to extinguish, but redirect him while experiencing the bounds of his power.

My arrival startles him and at once our struggle ensues. Each maneuver reveals his skill, honed by years of gamesmanship at home and abroad. His reflexes are primal—his strength at its apex when our match begins. He is unsure of his adversary's identity—the likely assumption is that I am his brother.

An opportunity to seek the advantage comes into focus: he lacks flexibility. His body has stiffened from housing untended anger, sealed by young trauma grown old inside of him. His memory holds frozen images of a rage-filled Esau—steeped in Laban's thievery. These mix with his fermenting shame: "How could I have betrayed my twin; stolen from him what was his? Of course he wants to kill me!" His recollections pressed down by time stoke his anxiety. I am reminded my people's future is at stake…he cannot flee.

I grow weary and he must get on with his journey. One last blow unwinds his hip like a scroll; he winces from pain unspeakable, yet he does not let me go. I grant him a new name before he releases me. It is a gift, although he will see no benefit in that now.

How he will face Esau with such a debilitating limp, much less run for his escape, much less sit to relieve himself is a mystery to him. But even in his exhausted state, he is soon to realize there is no way around his travail, only through. This is the beginning of Israel's courage and my Preparation.

‡

SAMARITAN WOMAN

I Am Water

She refuses to look at me. With lowered head and hurried step, she avoids my gaze. With one glance, and then another, she urges me to move along. Palpable is her frustration as I linger in her spot and wait. She is wary; understandably so.

This is the one place she returns to day after day, away from the scorn of her neighbors. Outside of town, this stone on the well's edge is her only solace. She barely allows herself to drink while she steals away these forbidden moments.

My request for a drink confuses her. Offering a curtly challenge, she would rather discontinue conversation. But she has enough pity on this Pilgrim to offer her cup with the broken handle. She holds it like a treasure; it is all she has left of her mother. She would never forget her stepdaughter's carelessness with it. Never again would she let it out of her sight.

She has suffered at the hands of her husbands. With minimal prospects she is vulnerable prey to their seductions. I know her secrets; I know about him, the one she thinks she has kept hidden. I know the little ones lost, her body too damaged by the brutality that came before. I see what they do not: her untapped brilliance, the brightness her sorrow veils. Wearing shame like her tattered tunic, she cloaks her Self to hide, elude. No one expects much of her any more. Her drawing inward has worn them out. That is her plan as she lives out her days, to be left alone to ponder why she remains. If this meaninglessness prevails, what matters of life?

But buried deep resides yearning for a life liberated. She thinks it would be easier for her if I left her to it, but I mean to share my true identity with her; she will be the first to know it fully.

What will she do?

I am Parched

He tells me his secret—how can it be? It is hope beyond hope. And how can this be happening here, on this spot, on this day? To me?

I try to shrug him off at first. Despite my efforts, he persists in speaking with me. One cannot trust a Jew who talks to a woman like me, I am unclean-of-the-unclean; all are repulsed by me. Scrape as I have, there is nothing to redeem me from the dregs of my people. I am used up and hollow, like chaff to be blown by the summer wind.

For many years I came here to pray for a child—like Jacob's Rachel. Alas, I am cursed, unable to bear. Those days are behind me now, scarred over and dry. I have taken up my husband's children; fed them, cleaned them, loved them, to no avail—all I have known is their contempt. After all, I was never the mother they longed for. Long ago I made peace with my loneliness to keep it from devouring me—besides mother's cup, it has become my only comfort.

So there it is. He should not even talk to me...

The only way I know he is True: he knows everything about me. He knows about them all, about him, the one I love but keep hidden. He is plain in his statements—they are facts after all. But his voice lacks the judgment of the others. While they retreat, he remains with kindness and warmth like I have never known. Somehow, it seems he understands.

If it is so, that He Is who He Is, I must go tell the others. They will not know to come here. This is not their well. Surely if he knows me, he knows them...

‡

JONAH

I am Jonah

Where is the justice? You cannot be unaware of what these Ninevites have perpetrated on neighbors and countrymen alike! Why would all consequence be removed? Why would You reconcile them to a peace so undeserved?

Were my days in the putrefied belly of the beast a trifle? This is exactly why I ran from Your insistence to come here. I knew You would preserve them from paying their rightful debt. You have wiped the ledger clean—and what do I have to show for it?

And what is my reward for sacrificing these years for an enemy of my people, Your supposed chosen? Scorching desert heat? I loathe You! Would that I might be reclining against my father's olive trees rather than this withering vine in a barren wilderness! And why tease me with the shade of one day only to punish with the exposure of the next? You show those wretches your mercy but none remains for me, Your messenger? Ha! Your favor is fickle—it has engulfed me like the fish, only to spit me out in this reviled land, my body burned raw from entrails and bile.

Where is that cursed worm? How can such a small creature destroy my only cover against these elements? This proves You have no care for me; I welcome death rather than a future. It would have been better for me to perish.

Jonah, has not a shred of your living death stayed with you? What is this anger? Did your vow to Me mean nothing? Am I to answer to the whims of your entitlement for having saved you? Do you seek some reward beyond your very life?

And what would you have Me do, Jonah? What are your designs? Because I have elevated your usefulness, do you now think My love should be withheld from these? You understand little to nothing. Your bitterness blinds you.

How I long for you to share in My joy as this wayward people return home. They will further My purposes to surrounding nations. They will be My beacon! Your part in their restoration is somehow insufficient for your agenda. It is of great sorrow to Me that you have forgotten, Jonah—I fear you will not remember the truth of My unfailing kindness. What tragedy to have embraced a people, but lost a son.

He is not lost, this prodigal. After all, he has returned to do Your bidding and he is weary. This, his elder season and he is alone in a despised land. The shade, his only reminder of Your care, is a paltry substitute for the comforts of home to which he longs to return.

We have shaped and formed him, and so it is right that You want him to grasp the greatness of Your work in these people—You believe he can. You have given him Your vision and so he sees, but as a function of his broken body and the obedience You forced upon him, he now wants rest—his eyes are weak and mired in regret. He is spent beyond his resources and cannot understand why this is too much to ask.

Can you see his scars? Who lives through their body's own decomposition? Only One-Other; I have lived within the confines of his frailty, faced the physical suffering. I carry his sign as a testament to his nights of howling desperation, cocooned in the entrails of Your great fish, only to hear Your silence. A refining fire indeed—no cauldron can match that bilious tomb.

Jonah is my cautionary tale. To live in constant surrender to the demands of Beyond brandishes exhaustion mixed with unanticipated invincibility. The need for relief, disguised as Your design, takes over. This is survival, it is preservation. I will want said relief, over and over.

‡

MARY, MOTHER

I am Mother

It is agonizing to release him to his fate, not to speak of the daily struggle to share him with Him, the God of my fathers. My much awaited son; his earthly end has been kept from me until this final season. This is grace, as it would have been too much to bear along the way. The constant foreboding is enough.

He is my firstborn. Joseph was forgiving given the surreal circumstances of our marriage. He bore up under it all, but it was not the dream we had imagined—the disruption wore on us both. More children would come, yet none fill his shoes, and I am sure they sense it.

In many ways, we are each other's. Birthing God-in-the-flesh-of-my-son brought many fears while his divine imprint wrought an insatiable appetite for him—how can I not turn towards him for anything, everything? My intuition a heavy burden, I have smothered him with protection. He was early to most successes, bearing a mind to understand his Origins, and therefore, his earthly demise. It was early that I learned to contain my anxiety when I could. I have tried.

It is a privilege to know what I know and see what I see, and in spite of all, travel this path. The whole of my people's story rests upon him, and he carries this with solidity. But now I see sadness emerging from what is required of him. I have felt distance between us, so I am relieved that he consented to attend the wedding and bring a few friends with him. He is somewhat of a loner; I am encouraged that others will join him. I long for him to be closer to his siblings—a mother's love holds endless yearnings for a family never meant to be. Our fractures might shatter us all with any more strain. He knows this too well.

I am eager to see him, especially in Joseph's absence. His greeting is pleasant enough, but with notable inwardness. It takes every bit of effort not to cling and question: "How are you? Is something wrong? If so, is it me? What can I do?" I try to celebrate with old friends, but am easily distracted—wondering where he is, how does he look, who he is talking to, does he miss me? Are his friends worthy of his time? They are working-class, not the studied elite with whom he seemed most compatible until recently. Just back from a pilgrimage of some kind, he appears gaunt from his fasting, a little more serious than usual, but engaging nonetheless. My friends know of our scandalous beginnings. I can tell they, too, are curious and observing.

Doesn't every wedding celebration hold an opportunity for drama? The father-of-the-bride, in a state of panic, finds me: "There is no more wine, what are we to do?"

My body moves before my thoughts can form. "Where's Jesus?" I ask. Someone unknown to me points and I move swiftly. I know I must ask him. I understand how this is to be solved.

His eyes meet mine; he knows before I utter words that I am about to make a request of him. This time I cannot restrain, for our hosts' humiliation is imminent. The only words I can muster: "They have no more wine."

I Am Son

She is formidable.

She can see right through me, there is no hiding from her, and yet I cannot share what is coming. How could she stand it?

Her love stifled me—mine was a traumatic entry that would seal our earthly bond. To avoid public scorn, ours became a quiet struggle and a secret to many. In a sense I came before Joseph—although he knew who I was and was kind in his care for me. He taught me his craft, although I lacked the skill and the want for it. I know that disappointed him. I wish to tell him more about my future and my gratitude for his provision. It was not easy for him. I saw the importance of him in my studies—if not for him there would be no Way for his people.

I will protect her from what is solely mine to face. I am equipped for my end as she was for my beginnings in this world. In some way, I wish it were part of my Purpose to please her. She is well intentioned, but she will not see what needs seeing. My parting gift is to bend to her request, for she has suffered enough, and there is more to come. Her friends' praise is her small consolation.

JESUS

I Am Cast Out

My studies with Rabbi revealed me to my Self—a welcome relief from my younger years, filled with gnawing hunger for my true Origins. He took notice of my proficiency with both language and understanding of my human lineage, although none could know the full nature of my quest. The Prophets knit together strands of reason for my existence and coming suffering. Their teaching took root—but living this frail existence cultivated those seeds of knowing like no amount of study ever could.

The arc of my forefathers' journey yielded an important discovery: my people could not retain Truth for prolonged periods. They would forget to remember, blinded often by impulse, uncertainty, or hardship. Holding this Truth through daily practice was at the heart of this life's struggle. I can sympathize now; it is effort to stay clear and connected to Unwavering Love for my Self and my Purposes, especially when there is rejection; and there is always that.

I return home following the baptism by John and the desert wandering that came after, eager to share what else I have learned about my Self with those I love most. Drawn to the synagogue, my home-away-from-home, I am invited to read from the sacred text. While depleted, I hear the centering Truth in my own voice and it invigorates me—feeling once again to my core, I AM.

As I read, I sense their unease. These people know me, and have known me, but cannot stretch to see me as their Healer and Ransom Payer. I remember the words of an ancient forebear: "A prophet has no honor in his home town". I speak these words before my thoughts complete them: "Surely you will say that a physician must heal thyself." These indictments inflame them. They must reduce me to a previous version of myself to satisfy. I AM the mirror reflecting their failure to see clearly.

Theirs is a vehement rejection. Their shock exposes them—I do not fit within their timing. They feel they should have known sooner. They only see me as Joseph's son.

At once I am outside the temple, driven out by their blind rage and their will to deny whom they should love. I know not to chase them into belief as they insist I only blaspheme. So quick to descend into violence, I must leave and release them to their fate as I am released to my own. There are others who will see.

‡

HEMORRHAGING WOMAN

I am Daughter

It seems there are no answers for my condition. The prodding and concoctions of various healers have accomplished nothing; save to line their pockets with whatever I could pay. Even my husband can hardly look at me. He has become like those who scoff when I pass by. He will leave me soon. Perhaps he has already.

Every covering is soiled; I am forced to wear what rags I have left. The hours spent at the river's edge tending the stains are nothing but futile. I scour and wring, only to be standing in it once again. To feel clean, to wear a fresh garment; these are the stuff of fantasy. There is nothing to dry and absorb. Yes, it is gruesome! Yes, they all turn away! They can be nothing but disgusted—I disgust my self!

I dare not remember what I was like before this blood. I avoid my reflection—it belies the drain—colorless eyes, pallid skin, my wan expression. I must hold some hidden flaw that requires this continual dousing. Some blackness within demands I must be cleansed. I am confessor and blood sacrifice in one.

My neighbor takes pity on me. She brings soap from the market and occasionally leaves a worn tunic on my threshold. Yesterday, she brought word of a traveling healer—most likely another charlatan. She says he is Expected, which only means the entire village will turn out for him, all craving some diversion from the emptiness that consumes us. Their agenda is of no consequence as desperate as I am for this womb to close. What would it be like to walk and move without this dripping nightmare?

With my heartless taskmaster ever my companion, the night spent in the town square was all the more daunting. Plagued by its need to gush, there was no sleep, no disguising the flow. Perhaps an omen; it might know I intend to pursue its end today.

"Have your way with me this one last time!" This is why I am the town outcast; I have been reduced to talking to my self.

News of his arrival interrupts the conversation—now he is just outside the city gate! How will he know that mine is not just a wound that requires dressing? And how will I get to him? Why haven't I thought that through? If I stand now and run to him the shame will swallow me whole. His refusal is my dread. I am prepared for that; I will walk into the river where the water is high and yield to the current, never to return. That would be a better end to this living death.

No wonder the rumors! He is unmistakable even from a distance. He draws closer while more and more descend to catch their glimpse, or plead for a slice of healing. I wish I could run to him, but they would surround me and keep me from making him unclean, and then the brutality would follow. To them I am a contagion to be stamped out.

I will crawl and risk the trampling. That will be reason enough for the blood should they find my corpse. Perhaps only a few will remember the truth. I fall to my knees to begin my slithering approach, camouflaged by the blood-mottled dust. I might reach him just as the wave of people crashes around him, leaving enough room to brush the edge of his cloak. That is all it would require! He need not even see me.

I inch ever closer, the dust absorbing the flow, while leaving my path evident for all. The bruises of each kick will be my trophies for weeks to come, but my eyes remain on each footfall. There it is! I see the hem floating above his sandal, and by some miracle the tips of my fingers just glance the frayed threads as he moves past, completely unaware of my presence, or so I hope. I will lie here until the dust settles, then run to the river to wash and see whether anything has transpired. I barely allow myself this seed of hope that something of another place roiled through me—but it could have been that just another swift kick landed perfectly.

Why have they stopped? What are they gawking at? Where is the hole deep enough for my retreat? What is he saying to me? Why would he be speaking to me?

I Am Expected

The crowd presses in and I am caught by its stifling need. Like a riptide, it pulls me under and spits me out down the road apiece. As I resurface, I try to catch my breath and concentrate on the soles of my feet feeling their way through, steadying the pace. No help can be given if I am not within my Self today.

To many, I am a spectacle, or prophet-of-the-moment. Whatever they need me to be is no matter. They are oppressed from all sides, and change within is difficult. To be awake in their lives is to take stock of what is against them. And I do not make it easy for them; my parables are rife with double meanings. If they have heard of the healings or miracles, they will come to partake or to scrutinize, to witness or spy— but very few will believe I am Expected. And even fewer will follow beyond their met need today.

I sense an approaching presence; some serpentine form nipping at my heels beneath the litter of needy pups. At once I am pulled to my inner depths as my energy flees my body. My curiosity is piqued within my disorientation; I must lay eyes on whoever broke through the throng. Who is this persistent soul?

Ah, there she is. I knew it was a woman! Her determination reminds me of my mother's will. Her touch indicates that she knows without yet knowing. My mind's eye sees her womb closing, no longer a leaky cistern. She is fearless to have ventured toward me on the ground. To dust she returned, and from dust she is transformed. She, of course, doubts anything has occurred, she prepares her hopes to be dashed as they have been so many times before. She is eager to depart to the river, to wash and examine her self.

They urge me to move on, paying her no mind. But she has been passed over long enough—they cannot see beyond her uncleanliness. To heal the essence of one is worth more than one hundred cures. Let the record show the surety of her belief. Through me, she has gathered her power back and now, she can rest. She has suffered enough, dear daughter. The prayer of her blood has been answered.

‡

NICODEMUS

I am Nicodemus

Like moth to flame I am drawn to his wisdom.

His soul is ancient, yet he speaks of young mind, young mind, always the children. What could this mean? The Prophets never speak of this.

I visit him in the shadows of the night. It is not wise to be seen with him now, he is under suspicion. My superiors will question—I must be ready to give an answer for my whereabouts, that is why I am here under cover of darkness. If I am discovered, my position will be in jeopardy. Caiaphas feels threatened by this Teacher like none other—his restlessness will give way to slaughter and I would rather not be part of the fray.

So, flesh-on-bone, Teacher, give me something to hold on to, not this elusive talk, or these impossible concepts. Give me enough so that I may protect you from what is coming. Am I too old to understand? Do you not trust me?

I Am Secret

In quiet whispers you may hear me. Or, you may not. Almost silent, I stalk, I haunt. "Prey, listen", is my refrain. You retort: "Not now, I am too busy with this or that".

Distraction is often chosen instead of the stillness my volume requires. I demand an audience. But I am one of many seeking the center of your soul's stage. I will not compete.

Will your fear overtake you and keep you from knowing me? Because there may be a cost, or unintended, even lasting, consequence. It is true, the Way is narrow, but welcome to all. But all do not choose it, you know this. You know there are others who will not want to travel this path, perhaps even those you dearly love. And this devastates you. You think your Self too weak for the loneliness—but life is riddled with it. Make peace with it soon.

What is at stake? It is too difficult to reason with you, for your quest is about the business of politics, your high priest, the prefect, Rome's rule—for these are desolate times, I do not envy your position. You walk the knife's blade.

So, Nicodemus, tuck me in the folds of your garment for now, for you mistake sacrifice for scarcity. This is why you need rebirth, to shed your fear, to share your secret. Instead, you will hold me too long, as light under a bushel, never to be known.

‡

JOHN THE BAPTIST

I am Cousin

I wonder in these moments what they think of me, my parents long gone now. My doubt sneaks in on me like the mice in my cell, nibbling at the edges of my resolve, my clarity, my memory.

According to Herod I am safe in his prison. Not so, and not for long, and neither is he. Against my counsel, he married his brother's wife and now he is trapped in her vise. Like the wheat that blows in the summer wind, we wait to be cut down and milled to complete her recipe, to be served at her feast for power.

How I long for the days of my walkabout life to take me away from this drama. Cut loose to be fostered in my wilderness homeland by those who taught me how to channel my energy, which exhausted my dear parents. I quickened their departure, so late was my arrival to their lives. They had little strength left to harness me. So they let me go.

The caves were my scribes, their walls my scrolls, their symbols my language. Escaping the heat of the day to recline in their cool hovels, I would hear whispers of the Expected One, whispers that He was my cousin-in-the-flesh. I thought this a rumor until that day at the river's edge.

By then, I was considered a caveman pot-stirrer, heralding the news: One was coming. The promise of His arrival had become my food, my drink. Along with the locusts, the message was my sustenance. Unencumbered by the trappings of convention, I was ready to initiate. That was my role as I understood it, and that was my singular focus.

I dream of that day even now: He appears from the thicket with an aura of deepest knowing. A seamless interlude of dance-like movements ensues as He enters the water. My arms become branches that lower His head until it is immersed in the flow.

In the current, I see that His life's river will move Him forward into great challenges: sacrifice, friendship, success, oppression, loneliness, alienation, rejection, defeat, betrayal, fear unto trembling, grief, despair, celebration, death and triumph. He is to experience it all, nothing withheld. Why else would He have come?

The race had begun long before, and while He had trained for it well—in fact, He was prodigious—the home stretch would test and try Him beyond His studies. Living through would deplete His reserves— He would pull from something deeper within to endure. But this was unclear to Him this day—this was only His beginning.

This dream of a memory is all I have left, it is all that remains. It leaves me too quickly, I wish I could hold on to it in this forsaken place where there is no comfort. At times, when quiet overtakes me, I listen for Voice. He boomed unmistakable that day, never to be forgotten, shaking us to the core.

Perhaps He will respond to my letters. While Herod prods me to question His identity, and every now and again, I fall prey to it, my hope is that He can read between these lines and know that I know and think of Him often. His journey will soon come to a close, although I know not when. I fear I will beat Him to it.

I AM Voice

I remember. I AM your dream:

You pull Him through the veil and His eyes drift upwards. He shakes them of their liquid residue to see what flies towards Him from above. You both startle at my announcement: "You are Mine, You are Loved."

I feel His heart fall through His stomach while you stare at the clouds like Ezekiel. Surprised as He was by His desperation for My Voice, My validation, He never would have asked for it. I knew what was to come—this declaration was meant to sustain Him—especially through the desert sifting just before Him.

I had been quiet until then, except through the text of His studies and the love of His family. He waited in hope to hear from Me more directly. But I chose My timing carefully. His passing through the symbolic waters of death to life was His clear acceptance of the mission, and I could hardly contain My relief. After all, He could have refused to walk the narrow path before Him. Threshold crossed—it had begun.

Kindred, you have done well to fulfill your part in making the Way ready. You are not forgotten, forerunning in life and in death. Your bitter end approaches, it will be brutal and swift. I await your arrival.

‡

MARY OF BETHANY

I am Sister

I see it in your eyes, the dreaded passage before you. You have spoken of it before, perhaps only seeing a glimpse of it. Your gaze lingers on me for a moment, and then you are gone; sights fixed on your final earthly perch.

How Martha toils for this, your living wake. Recline here; conserve your strength. I know this is to be our final gathering—the turning tide will scatter us all for a time. Terror comes to us for knowing you, much less loving you. Dread upon dread.

The breaking glass startles you at first, but at once you know exactly what I am about to do. My sorrow presses me to your feet, bottle in hand, and I am undeterred by their barbs. This is my parting gift to you; I pray the lasting aroma will hold momentary relief as you begin to traverse the depths. You are my anchor; it is my turn to be yours.

Kindred spirit, brother-friend, how can I let you go? Another will never fill the void you leave. I will try to trust what you have said—that you will be with me in other ways. You have confided in me that this time was approaching, and now your departure falls upon me like a dark curtain, with suffocating blackness.

I unwind my hair, remove your sandals, and slowly unfold from my collapse, stretching toward your torso, your head. Your eyes catch mine, filled with longing and gratitude. I feel the brewing storm just beneath your familiar serenity. Your breath is shallow, your chest heaving, but your anguish eases slightly with every touch. I know you knew this was coming, but to surrender to the nearing end proves difficult.

There is a silent agreement between us: these are our last shared moments together. You must know that you hold the depth of my soul and take it to your death and whatever comes after. Our friendship is my most cherished treasure. To honor your memory I will try to recover something of a life after losing you, but I will never forget.

I Am Brother

I have no energy for their shortsighted wonderings—bickering like siblings for their place at the table. They have had their time and yet now they fight over me. They are dear to me, however frustrating. Can they not see I need from them some steadfastness? Some courage?

And then, the brush of your hair at my feet brings me back from the abyss that yawns before me. You remove the gritty remains from my dusty journey. I know this is your preparation for my bitter end and your generous gift. Your touch reminds me not to depart just yet—stay present, if possible, a little longer. You care nothing for their glowering—they have always envied our closeness. There is no hesitation in your sweeping movements. Would that the others approach me with such assurance in the face of scrutiny.

The meal your sister has lovingly prepared is her share of the burden. Like you, she knows, but she can hardly face me without breaking apart. Her busyness is her distraction for now. It is just as well, for any more tenderness shown would unravel them.

You have already experienced this with Lazarus, just fresh from his grave. You know firsthand what I need, courageously preparing my body. You wash away the heaviness of the moment, so I can catch my breath. I am grateful to you for this extravagance, I know it was a great sacrifice to procure such a luxury. Their ire will turn towards you, this intimacy unsettles them. They are too busy puffing up, vying for special favor. They don't know how to make sense of it.

I feel your agony, akin to losing your brother. I do not want to leave you. You have grounded me throughout this challenging season—enduring it has exacted a surprising toll. I hold dear our times together, our walks, our conversations. You are family of my heart, respite from the strain. At this threshold to my darkest hour I will carry with me the aroma as your presence. I will always remember you.

JUDAS

I am Traitor

Searching for it, I have found the tree that will serve me well this evening.

I have thrown in with the darkness that haunted me as a child. I can no longer outrun it, it has caught me. How could I have done it?

Why? So tired from wanting, from the lack that also haunted. I was ravenous, the runt of ten children, my parents never knowing when or how to stop rutting—the number of us was the only thing that ever flourished by their hands. A tribe, yes, but a tribe of ne'er-do-wells.

It was sheer torture to be in charge of our group's treasury, meager to some, but to me, a lost inheritance found. One might say my upbringing brought with it a necessary creativity, and so, I had done my best to invest wisely, while just enough found its way into my pockets to numb the hunger for a moment. I didn't know then what I now know with certainty…no amount would satisfy this ache. It is still with me, even with the fee paid and pouch jangling. I should be relishing the prize—thirty pieces of anything is more than I have seen in a lifetime.

Do it in secret, this scheme. That's what I told myself, that no one would discover my plot, my manipulations. Here's the catch: He is the Seer of all Seers, and He knows me better than I know myself. His light would not only illuminate my darkness, it would carve and sear its way inside, scorning me all the while. The burn chafed and angered me. I was drawn to it and loathed it simultaneously. This often paralyzed me. He called this Love, this foreign current, and I dreaded its surfacing and focusing in on me. Let my dark corners be, is that too much to ask?

The tipping point: when she broke that bottle of nard over His head, all I could see was the waste, a year's worth of wages lost in a moment. And He savored it, and publicly shamed me for suggesting it be sold for the poor. For the poor! That is where I wanted the money to go! Once liquidated, there would be plenty for all!

Remorse takes hold and now strangles. I hadn't expected it! The noose I fashion will be welcome relief. If it does not do the trick, surely the bough will break and complete the task. Beyond recognition, that's what I desire.

I am Shadow

I have turned you, Judas, and protected you until you succeeded in my plans. While whispering lies of grandiosity, my forked tongue poked those pesky wounds of yours, infecting with envy, ripening with greed. Like a gourd, I have hollowed out any seeds of promise. You are my progeny, not His. He will lose two sons between sunrise and sunset. At least I have won this prize: His day of pure sacrifice will be tainted by your infamy.

Where is your doting Father now? You have been played for a fool, Judas. Indeed, you are Cain-incarnate, instrument of death to precious Son, with one exception, you could never bear the fate of a vagrant wanderer, you haven't the stomach for it, I have seen to that.

I cannot help what happens next: bottomless wanton awaits you. From here you will be left to your own imprisonment, no rations, nothing to spare. Unending starvation. Drowning in your own waste. Eternal heat, grinding down, filing you to nubby flesh. Sifting beyond existence. Beneath words, all of it. You will know soon enough, my son.

Welcome home.

I Am Father

It need not end this way, Judas. You are not the first, nor the last of many who will refuse entry to the Light. But it is not too late, even for you.

Your twisted vision keeps you from seeing outside of your jealousy and resentment. Your scraping yields a fraction of what is possible. You grip too tightly your emptiness. You fancy yourself a dark leader. Yet you will be devoured like all others before you unless you listen to the still small voice that cries out within you to soften, humble yourself, return, recover. This is all yours to accept, can't you see it?

You have until your very last breath and even beyond that. Even until that moment when your body gives up its consciousness to its next destination. I fear you are resigning yourself to prowl like those lost before you. No rest, no belly full, eternal exile. While you are son of Adam, you are also son of Cain—your pride-covered cowardice comes first. You have taken life not yours into your own hands, and now His blood cries out to me.

You think you are the only one to suffer at the hands of folly and brokenness? Such is the path of all humanity. You have believed the lie of your victim, but your truth can still overcome. I fear you will take the easy route, the comfortable, the destructive. To be fulfilled is too daunting, too unknown. Your clever manipulation in the hands of your goodness would heal you, Judas, despite your egregious crimes.

The sins of your father's father set this in motion—lineage of neglect left you to feed your darkness untended. It is their pattern, their habit meant to be challenged by you, your generation. Why leave it to another? This was your mission! Your time!

Remember your grandmother's embrace? Her prayers were sewn into the fibers of your being. When your father allowed her near you she would shine her light into the dark pockets of your soul—and for a moment, you would thrive, unfolding beneath her warmth. She saw your promise yet unformed.

You have persevered through much, Judas. But you have turned towards cruelty leaving your heart a craven wasteland. It only requires Love's tending to flourish your seed of goodness. This is why I linger, I am here to gather you up and help you set things a right.

I fear this is all for naught. I see your end approaching. I cannot reach you, this is your choice. But I will remain until your final moment, there is still time.

The bough breaks, the sparrow falls just beyond My grasp. I waited until the last, Judas. My heart remained open, My hand extended. With your shattered body breaks My heart, Judas, and with it all possibility for repair. You carry a piece with you. The knowledge of what could have been between us will crush you again and again, as it will Me.

‡

JESUS

I Am Sent

I now see that we have much in common, Jacob and I. Through traumatic birth, and a mysterious father, we became our mothers' favored sons. In time, after toiling in my father's carpentry business, I risked rejection from my birth family when I left to follow my calling. Having dashed their hopes for me to carry on Joseph's legacy, they lived in fear of their own rejection for my decision, with all of its implications.

Like Jacob, I traveled to the river's edge to meet my cousin, unknown to me, waiting expectantly for my arrival. He saw in me what I could not yet see in myself and bathed me in his knowing water. You affirm for the first time in thirty long years with the sign of the dove as You promised. It buoyed me as I left that wilderness for yet another, inhospitable to me in every way.

Forty days I searched the skies for another dove while I faced my desert foe. He devoured me with tricks perpetrated for generations on Your beloved people. The torment rushed to me and through me and I felt it for all, for Jacob, for Me, for You. No hunger, or thirst will ever rival his savagery. And yet, this was only the beginning, our first round.

Like Jacob, I now know betrayal. It came from a brother who knows me better than most. I was taught to expect it, but it has nonetheless crushed me at a most critical hour. My opponent eagerly awaits our final match—his wilderness defeat has only sharpened his treachery.

To finish the gauntlet laid before me requires both courage and surrender. I have the power to fight, and wonder why this cannot somehow be undone. I remember in Jacob's eyes I caught a glimpse of his pain, his want to hold on, his will's refusal to be shattered, while my body breaks under this brutality. I plead to be rescued, but know I must ultimately submit to my own destruction for the sake of greater transformation. It is what must be.

But like Jacob, I feel alone at the edge of this deep—even You have abandoned me, or so it seems. My family and friends hover, tethered though disconnected from me—my peril is beyond comprehension. None pierce the isolation that has become like skin. I have mastered the essence of suffering: when we need most, we are left to face what only we must face. There is no one else who can, not even You. You know suffering, but You will not live it like this, and any comfort You offer would feel fleeting. Perhaps this is why You stand silent witness instead, allowing me to become their representative. You must know that loving intention does not quench the longing for some tangible version of You in these dire moments. I will remind You on their behalf.

Two strangers accompany me to my harrowing end. One is overtaken by pain, longing for death to steal him as he has stolen, while one utters profession through bloody breath. He and I will walk our dying path together. My last moments reveal that I Am Sent, if only for this friend, as I was Sent to Jacob at the river's edge many years before.

‡

SIMON

I am Simon

He named me Peter.

Rough-hewn He found me, to my family's chagrin, a miserable excuse for a fisherman. Too serious and brooding for the task, my griping would repel my catch, and so, there was never enough to speak of.

Life on the water wasn't for me, I knew this always, but my father insisted. His will was stronger than mine. As brash as I am, he is the only man I feared, until Him. Never nimble, I lacked the patience to become a fisherman of merit. The Sea always flourished, but no matter the efforts, I would come up wanting. I was bored with the prospect and craved a new challenge, but was convinced none would find me in that backwater place. So I was destined, or better, resigned to this fate: I would never amount to much.

Imagine my surprise when He found me that day lamenting over an empty net that needed mending. By then, I was the Sea's laughingstock; I thought Him to be a newcomer who had already bested me in numbers. Instead, He presented an invitation of sorts—to use my skills in another venue altogether.

He seemed to come from a far off place, yet was reminiscent of a boyhood friend returned home; a familiar stranger. He spoke of a plan, a grand plan, really, a laughable plan. How does one bait a hook to catch a man? Amused but doubtful, I am not sure why He would have seen me as helpful. It was not as if I was well liked, or held any stature outside of my father's influence. My brother was always favored, so it made sense to choose him. I was the also-ran to be sure.

But a flicker of excitement caught somewhere in my soul as He unfurled His ideas. He already had His end in sight, so it seemed. This remained with me throughout: His focus, His directness, His kindness, His laughter in spite of knowing the coming horror. What they would do to Him is beyond description. Unthinkable. Too difficult to witness. I would flee those, His darkest moments, when He needed me most. That I was absentee still nags at my conscience—I fear I will never get past it, this regret is my constant companion. I wonder how I ever contributed to the cause. There are days when all I can see is my failure. My success too often one step from defeat, like that fabled night on the water, or my nightmare in Gethsemane.

To this day, I know not why He selected me, bumbler that I was, saying the wrong thing at the wrong time, wavering in my belief in Him. He was sure to call me on my short sightedness, caring enough to be firm with me and keep me from hindering His path. There were moments I thought I knew better than Him. How could I? How stupid.

But, I was strong, and loyal. My brooding would morph into confidence under His nurture. Somehow, He saw fit to rename me. Somehow, I know not how, I became His rock and we became friends.

The way I keep Him close is to throw off the cloak of guilt that hovers and speak of Him without hesitation at the gate called Beautiful—to speak the truth of what was done to Him, knowing full well that He knew all along what would happen. These are my glory days—confidence oozes from every pore of my being, words flow like honey from the comb, complete with bee's sting, leaving its welt again and again.

He spoke once of our sharing an earthly demise. It was a passing comment brought on by fruitless competition between us. I now know the inside of every prison in the vicinity. Jails cannot hold me, they are hole-filled nets and I am their big fish, lost to their carelessness—they are bound to tire of me soon.

What comes next is the inevitable mystery. It will resolve itself soon enough. We flourish in the meantime.

Indeed, we have become fishers of men.

I Am Beautiful

As you are, Peter. You step through the gate that is my Name's sake and heal a man long-crippled, just as you allowed your Self to be transformed during our short time together.

You have bitten hard on the hook set for you. I saw your stalwart nature, understood your hunger for meaning. You took the bait when you were ready and through your faith became my friend to this day and beyond.

What was once stubborn in you is now relentless fervor for me. True, you encumber yourself with regret and mistake it for motivation, or some lack to overcome. You will contend with that throughout, it is just your way.

You knew me before most. From my earliest reckoning, I had hoped for a brother to travel with me. While your nature would frustrate, I saw your greatness when you took your first step onto the water. To see your shock and surprise humored me. I wanted you to know what was possible and what our connection made capable. Even in your denial, or your garden slumber, I was with you, however grieved. After all, you were not meant to carry the yoke that was mine only to bear.

We run together now, I in you, you in me, we are one. You no longer fight the tide of your calling, and so reap the benefits of miracles performed and delivered. Catch-and-release, you are the slippery fish that evades their grasp just as the Sea evaded yours. Your empty nets are now full. New waters call you; you swim with their current.

While your end remains a mystery to you, even in this, we are one. You will be caught and hung on a tree. You choose a posture of remorse to face down the dust of your origins. Your humility duly noted, your guilt will be left behind; it is not needed where you are going. You will see soon enough.

Brother, friend, I will meet you there at another Beautiful Gate to the place I told you about so many times.

‡

EPILOGUE

What is contained within these pages comes from a place of love: love for the vocation of psychotherapy; even more, love for those who have invited me to witness their innermost struggles. Treading such hallowed ground has in no small part inspired these renderings of scriptural characters at various crossroads. All of whom needed something Beyond themselves to weather the storms or stagnancy within their lives.

These particular characters have emerged as guides due to the universal nature of their challenges and their resilience, each transcending the bounds of time. They have left for those interested a record as relevant for today as ever. In fact, I would like to invite each to my office; I believe they would serve as highly effective co-therapists for client-seekers in our modern era.

May these frontiersmen and women somehow be a bridge to your own human journey; may their endeavors, both spiritual and emotional, serve as light, illuminating, maybe even deepening, your own connection to the Beyond within.

INSPIRATION

Jacob
Genesis 32:24-32

Samaritan Woman
John 4:1-45

Jonah
Jonah 1-4

Mary, Mother
John 2:1-11

Jesus
Luke 4:14-30

Hemorrhaging Woman
Mark 5:25-34

Nicodemus
John 3:1-21

John the Baptist
Mark 1:1-8, Matthew 11:1-19, Mark 6:14-29

Mary of Bethany
John 12:1-8, Matthew 12:38-41

Judas
Matthew 27:1-10, John 12:4-6, John 13:21-30

Jesus
Luke 23:33-46, Matthew 27:33-54

Simon
Acts 3-4

ACKNOWLEDGMENTS

Perhaps it goes without saying that my essential Hero is the Man around Whom these stories center. This is an insufficient tribute to His sustaining constancy.

Numerous others have contributed to this effort from its inception to completion. My heartfelt thanks to those who may not be mentioned here, but who, nonetheless, played a role in the creation of this collection.

As previously mentioned, to those seeking, and sometimes weary souls who have allowed me to share in this often painful and sobering human journey, your lives have taught me more than can be captured here. Thank you.

To Tim and Jane Sharp, my earliest mentors in the art of weaving together diverse creative and vocational pursuits, your home was the launching pad for the most significant events of my adulthood. Thank you for your expansive hospitality and kindness.

John Marshall, I am forever grateful that yours was the office I found once enough courage surfaced to request support at the most critical turning point in my life to date.

Don Harvey, your early belief in my abilities as a practitioner, combined with your deft capacity to teach the intangibles of the craft, established the foundation for a vocational life of meaning for which I remain most appreciative.

Louis McBurney and Donald E. Capps, you have left extraordinary wakes in your areas of expertise and you are missed. Thank you for your contribution to the early development of this work.

Acknowledgments

Donna Scott, Janet Salyer, Bea Scarlata, you are consummate feminine spiritual healers and guides, all extraordinary resources towards my personal healing.

Ataana Badilli, your vision helped me see what needed to be seen within and release what no longer belonged.

Kelly Falzone, you served as a therapist for my novice writer-self, regularly stymied by her inhibitions. Thank you for your insightful promptings to trust her wisdom.

Sandi Rice, this volume would be incomplete without your tenacious care and mobilizing guidance.

Dr. Shelia K. Littauer, your incisive and loving enthusiasm arrived at just the right time.

I would be remiss if I did not mention the literary voices whose breadcrumbs of wisdom provided nourishing inspiration when it was most needed. I could not more highly recommend their works to readers in search of handholds along their spiritual journey: Henri Nouwen, Reynolds Price, John Sanford, Donald E. Capps, Anita Saltonstall Ward, Jean-Yves LeLoup, Kahlil Gibran, Dorothy Sayers, and Eugene Peterson, to name a few.

Warm appreciation to early, thoughtful readers, both friends and family, whose poignant encouragement helped clear lingering moments of wondering: Rich Steinle, Mimi Omiecinski, Jill Bishop, Nataliya Mann, Yvonne Helf, Anne Frame, Kim Fournier, Danan Whiddon, Dudley Smith, Charlie McClendon, the River Rat Men's Retreat, Pat and Gail Hayes, Clare Grisham, Rachel Corum, Jane McCracken, the Women's Focus Group, Pam Johnson, Tom Collins, Elizabeth Brown, and Walt Fuller.

Acknowledgments

John Blase and Doug Mann, many thanks for your early and fervent advocacy, which put wind in my sails to continue on.

Monty Powell, thank you for your pivotal support of this project and for lending your production expertise to the audio recording. More than all of that, to you and Anna, a force of nature, I am most thankful for your enduring friendship.

Art Helf, I carry your love, humor and indomitable spirit with me.

Heartfelt gratitude for Trish Smith and Donna and Steve Renner, without whose friendship, love and confidence, the grit of life would frequently seem insurmountable.

To Phil and Karen Pirecki, friends who happen to be family, here's to many more years of shared memories together.

Scott Norton and Vincent Mason—how it is that you have entered my life with such love and grace is only surpassed by the joy and ease of our connection—a rare gift, which I dearly treasure. Scott, deep thanks for contributing your brilliant literary prowess, not only an invaluable resource, but icing on the cake.

To my family, our shared story has shaped my inner frame. To my mother, gratitude for passing down loves that I cherish to this day and beyond. To my brother and sister, I honor your resilience and strength, acquired in part within the laboratory of living and loving that was our childhood home.

To my nieces and nephews, Aspin, Dawson, Megan, Joshua, Abygail and Isabel, my hope is that this collection will somehow, someday, impart soulful encouragement to generate your brightest inner light.

Acknowledgments

Bruno, creating our living history together remains one of the very few things that truly matter to me—I cannot imagine life otherwise. Nor could I imagine it without our dog children, Skagit, Sophie, Buddy and Totem—whose love is the sweetest rounding out of everything.

And lastly, but certainly not least, to my father, Phillip Cherico, feet-of-clay intact, you spent of your self in ways I will continue to honor.

ABOUT THE AUTHOR

Jennifer Pirecki resides in Franklin, Tennessee, with her husband, Bruno, and their ridiculously spoiled Rhodesian Ridgeback, Totem.

www.jenniferpirecki.com

79588794R00071

Made in the USA
Columbia, SC
26 October 2017